SEA OF ...

POEMS

Kraftgriots

Also in the series (POETRY)

David Cook *et al*: *Rising Voices*
Olu Oguibe: *A Gathering Fear;* winner, 1992 All Africa Okigbo prize for Literature & Honourable mention, 1993 Noma Award for Publishing in Africa
Nnimmo Bassey: *Patriots and Cockroaches*
Okinba Launko: *Dream-Seeker on Divining Chain*
Onookome Okome: *Pendants,* winner, 1993 ANA/Cadbury poetry prize
Nnimmo Bassey: *Poems on the Run*
Ebereonwu: *Suddenly God was Naked*
Tunde Olusunle: *Fingermarks*
Joe Ushie: *Lambs at the Shrine*
Chinyere Okafor: *From Earth's Bedchamber*
Ezenwa-Ohaeto: *The Voice of the Night Masquerade,* joint-winner, 1997 ANA/ Cadbury poetry prize
George Ehusani: *Fragments of Truth*
Remi Raji: *A Harvest of Laughters,* joint-winner 1997 ANA/Cadbury poetry prize
Patrick Ebewo: *Self-Portrait & Other Poems*
George Ehusani: *Petals of Truth*
Nnimmo Bassey: *Intercepted*
Joe Ushie: *Eclipse in Rwanda*
Femi Oyebode: *Selected Poems*
Ogaga Ifowodo: *Homeland & Other Poems,* winner, 1993 ANA poetry prize
Godwin Uyi Ojo: *Forlorn Dreams*
Tanure Ojaide: *Delta Blues and Home Songs*
Niyi Osundare: *The Word is an Egg* (2000)
Tayo Olafioye: *A Carnival of Looters* (2000)
Ibiwari Ikiriko: *Oily Tears of the Delta* (2000)
Arnold Udoka: *I am the Woman* (2000)
Akinloye Ojo: *In Flight* (2000)
Joe Ushie: *Hill Songs* (2000)
Ebereonwu: *The Insomniac Dragon* (2000)
Deola Fadipe: *I Make Pondripples* (2000)
Remi Raji: *Webs of Remembrance* (2001)
'Tope Omoniyi: *Farting Presidents and Other Poems* (2001)
Tunde Olusunle: *Rhythm of the Mortar* (2001)
Abdullahi Ismaila: *Ellipsis* (2001)
Tayo Olafioye: *The Parliament of Idiots: Tryst of the Sinators* (2002)
Femi Abodunrin: *It Would Take Time: Conversation with Living Ancestors* (2002)
Nnimmo Bassey: *We Thought It Was Oil But It Was Blood* (2002)
Ebi Yeibo: *A Song For Tomorrow and Other Poems* (2003)
Adebayo Lamikanra: *Heart Sounds* (2003)
Ezenwa-Ohaeto: *The Chants of a Minstrel* (2003), winner, 2004 ANA/NDDC poetry prize and joint-winner, 2005 LNG The Nigeria Prize for Literature
Seyi Adigun: *Kalakini: Songs of Many Colours* (2004)

SEA OF MY MIND
POEMS

Remi Raji

Published by

Kraft Books Limited
6A Polytechnic Road, Sango, Ibadan
Box 22084, University of Ibadan Post Office
Ibadan, Oyo State, Nigeria
℗ 0803 348 2474, 0805 129 1191
E-mail: kraftbooks@yahoo.com

First published 2013

ISBN 978–978–918–116–2

= KRAFTGRIOTS =
(A literary imprint of Kraft Books Limited)

Dedication

In memory of Mother and Father
And in praise of love and land.

Other collections of poetry by Remi Raji

A Harvest of Laughters (1997)
Webs of Remembrance (2001)
Shuttlesongs America: A Poetic Guided Tour (2003)
Lovesong for my wasteland (2005)
Gather my blood rivers of song (2009)

Acknowledgements

Much appreciation to the first readers and audience of the poems in this collection, and to those institutions and organisers who have supported the presentation of some of the poems at different places and times: the 12th International Festival of Mediterranean Poetry (Palma de Mallorca, Spain), the Catalan Poetry Circle (Bar Horiginal, Barcelona, Spain), the 6th International Lviv Literary Festival (Lviv, Ukraine) and the Lyrikline Poetry Festival (Berlin, Germany), for performance; and the University of Ibadan, for special support. I wish to thank the following people for giving suggestions and providing queries: Tunde Omobowale, Obododimma Oha, Tolu Odebunmi, Ijeoma Abugu and Olayombo Raji-Oyelade.

Also, gratitude to Hanna Yanovska, Marcela Knapp, Annie Bats, Monica Rinck and Melita Aleksa Varga, for translations.

Author's Note

Although I take it for granted that each of the poems in this collection has its own life and should speak for itself, I hereby assert the indulgence of a brief reflection. In this age, poetry becomes more revolutionary by aligning itself to other arts and forms of performance. The poetic is also a function of the aesthetic. Poetry is method, poetry is rage; poetry is love, poetry is angst. It is the balance between the survival and carriage of linguistic finesse and as well the survival and sustenance of a spartan economy of details.

Poetry is the twinkle of any sensation derivable from the expression of abstractions. It is also sometimes the achievement of tangible actions, wherever possible. Yet, this is sadly also the age when every colourless word, stringed to the other culpable line, goes on the errand of poetic acclaim.

Above all, I also think that poetry is the empathy of the vital imagery in flight, after the emotion or in pursuit of the action. This is part of what I set out to do in the nutshell of the trained word.

Waves, ebbs and flows, a salient number of my words has been plucked from the tongue of rivers. Suffice to say that *Sea of my mind* is generated from a constant dialogue with self and society.

Remi Raji
Berlin, March 2013

Contents

Dedication 5
Other collections of poetry by Remi Raji 6
Acknowledgements 7
Author's Note 8

Introit 11
I have been a journey 12

I: Waves 13
The sojourner's pledge 14
Untold 15
I am the captured cock 16
The stranger's keeper 17
The god of poetry 18
Praying mantis 20
A simple request 21
Snapshot I-V 23
The road to Gombe 28
Kiagbodo 30
Ukrainian day 32
Lines from Palma de Mallorca 34
Kwansaba I: Lessons from a dream sequence 36
Soft bite 37
All of me is people 38
Intimation of a final departure 39

II: Ebbs 41
The poet 42
Echoes of absence 43
News from home 44
Our fragments 45

My country is bereaved 46
Three desperations 48
Sniper 49
This house full of noise 50
Run, country, run 52
It is you 53
Counterfeit 54
City of prose 55
We are the rage 56
At last poetry is on the streets 57
The fire next time 61
I have seen dead bones rise 62

III: Flows 63
Sea of my mind 64
I am the one you breathe 65
Now I compare you with the skin of rivers 67
Sky scenes 68
Your name is the perfume of night 69
River, take my heart 70
Breathing 72
I like your adverbs 73
Clinging 74
There is no beautiful poem like you 75
Abebi 76
I give you 77
Kwansaba II: for Eugene Redmond 78
Every. Thing. Matters. 79
Resolve 80
May the wind follow my plaintiff wish 81

Recessional 83
Kèngbè Ọ̀rọ̀/In the barrel of words 84

Introit

I've been a journey...

Some journeys are taken without travelling;
some travelling happen without journeying.

Forced, fated, or by volition,
our journeys are inflicted moments
of departure and return,
and the sojourner cannot be the same
he who goes by that name...
I have been a journey.

I have been a journey, sometimes pathfinder,
sometimes follower, I live the praise name of my father
and his father's father: legendary sojourner,
carver of a thousand dreams,
transformer of crooked woods into human forms.

I have been a journey.

I spend my years like the moon,
patient, and steady through these seasons
a walker on the road,
not knowing my destination sometimes,
but walking all the same, towards a dream.

I commit you, therefore, to the mind,
of motion and encounter, of shuttling between spaces,
the surprising activity of discovery,
of moving without moving,
and of knowing without knowing.

And I have been a journey...
I am the pleasures and pains of leaving and returning.

I
Waves

The sojourner's pledge

Arise my feet, do not go where the landscape suffers a rift
Do not hide, when the libation with earth is due, do not shift.

I make a pledge this day, to rekindle hope in the hard ground
To swim in dreams, breathe life, to find rhythm where a river is
found.

Untold

Like the canary forbidden to sing for a century,
Now freed, I want to burst into an ocean of songs

Once buried in silence,
Awakened to the gift of voices,
I have killed a conspiracy of impotence...
Tranquil now, afraid now, what my lips will spill...

My stomach wants to burst out of its spleen
I ate the guts of the sunbird
I swallowed the throat of the robin
And I am cursed to greet the morning in many colours

What the rainbow said to me, I will teach you
What the riverbird whispered to me, I will tell
There is a cliff in my voice, to ride all the tales I have heard
I am seated here, wondering how to put this seizure in words

I am seated, training my voice,
silenced once, wiser now
a gurgling warmth, a cavity full of tiny sensations
what will the first word be, what will my first be?

Perched, full-winged, sensate, and primed for the wind's kiss
What, when we meet again, what will the first word be?

I have come to your door, penitent, poised for your potent
prayer.

I am the captured cock

I am the captured cock
In a game of pecking hens and ducks
And goons, where bats without wings perch.

I am the silenced cock
Where roaches roam the land in noisy limbs
Where the mouse prances because the cat is poisoned.

I am the captured cock
I am the bound jaws of the hyena
I am orphaned to the crucible of crude calculus.

I am the catwalk of the lion.
The seduction of traps invites me,
the elephant, fired into the pit of dance,
I smell the sneer in the goitre of hunters.

And I become the compound of spells
Offspring of song, willed to the cloud's breath
Willed to plant thunder in the belly of cowards
I have embraced the wind of coming rains.

The stranger's keeper

I fall for the strangeness of first meetings.
My heart is made to run in labour of friendliness
I do not know between fan or foe
I am quick to go like the fly after the corpse
Quick to cling to the open sore of the bloodied buffalo
I am quick to pitch my tent with the sick
And damn the logic of the sane.
I come to you
as if we have met before
In the privacy of the elevator,
I greet you
even in the currency of the public toilet
as if we've been there before, waiting
waiting for something to happen in the century.
I am the blood of the stranger, the unknown comer
And when that rare smile rises like the sun
it touches me deep in the skin.

Yes, I fall for the strangeness of first and repeated meetings.

The god of poetry

The god of poetry works
        in wondrous ways
he cuts a babel of tongues
        among the horsemen of shit
he sets the gift of fire
        in the house of hunger
in the misty morning
        he gathers my blood
in an inferno of laughters;

my laughter turns pearl-
        black, like liquid gold,
my laughter is also the leaf
        of pain in the corn rows
of rusted dreams.

When it rains
        it is god's saliva
that needles my dryness;
        he fills my mouth with thunder
and earth's boils feel the fire...
        the god of poetry strikes
in thunderous ways;
        he brings blinding light
into the liar house
        he twists the thief's tongue
he strikes the fake oracle
        on the head.

Now the fires of confessions burn them all
        they who broke the diviner chain

I count their cries and lick their tears,
                         so crisp, so crocodile salty.

The god of poetry is my sweetener.

Praying mantis

The praying mantis strolls in the sun
The praying mantis goes to the market of dance
Her daughters say they do not see the rhythm in the wind
They say there's only an old shadow twitching in the dark.

The praying mantis dies in the twirl
carrying all her wares of swing to the end
Now the dancer's daughters have lost their waists
To doubt and debts in the deal of dance.

A simple request

Who will cleanse his sweat
by the dung beetle's soap
Or make a stew
with the watery oil of crabs?
Who will make her child's necklace
with the fertile beads of toads
Or pound her yams
in the woodpecker's mortar?

Bring the ashes,
bring the ashes for the earth to see...
bring the ashes of dead winds
I say to the one who insists that water burns like fire.

Bring the spine,
bring the spleen
bring the entrails of the ant
I say to the sorcerer who knows the shells of pregnant snails.

Bring the blood of the snail
bring the tail of the frog
bring, oh bring the hump of the snake
I ask the neck of the long calabash.

Bring the skeleton of the salt washed by the rain
bring the grunt of the pig after the guillotine
bring the heat of yesterday's sun...
I say, bring the full-froth foams of the stale wine.

And I will bring the dead silence of stinging bees.

Who will cleanse his sweat
by the dung beetle's soap
Or make a stew

with the watery oil of crabs?
Who will make her child's necklace
with the fertile beads of toads
Or pound her yams
in the woodpecker's mortar?

Snapshot

I
There is a noisy waking in the silence...

There is a noisy waking in the silence...
Men walk in the thickets of their thoughts
Some blessed to be thorns, some cursed to thrive.
The world runs a race on crooked limbs
And one deaf foot does not tell the other...

Snapshot

II
a thousand thicket of seeds

a thousand thicket of seeds
the birds who perch on my barn had enough
in their throats the brocade of songful crops
i know no hunger in the famine of words
i have swallowed a market of melodies.

Snapshot

III
i have swallowed the throat of the songbird

i have swallowed the throat of the songbird
my tongue is made to bless the land
my finger is supple with earth's waist
above, the sky is a cotton of colours
in the last breath of the rains, there you stand.

Snapshot

IV
in the last wink of the day, there you walk

in the last wink of the day, there you walk
the wide-eyed moon, the coral brightness...
the rivers run because they hear your steps
now there will be a gurgling beneath
creatures in combat in want in dream in desire in longing...

Snapshot

V
finally, the mountain will appear to you

finally, the mountain will appear to you
as the happy path, the valley of dreams
you will walk, away from the war game, with me
into the new ceremonies of light and love.
Even the birds are singing differently, because of you.

The road to Gombe

The road to Gombe
Is filled with the certainties
Of potholes
Past Keffi,
past Gitata,
Past Jagindi, and Tasha...

Past Zankan,   .
Past Gadabiyu
Godogodo, Gidan Waya, Atuku Gada, Dogo Fili,
Antang, Nisama, Kanufi, Denji, Mailafiya,

By day
I know the names of districts
by the mathematics of petrol huts and prayer stations,
By night
the fireflies are soldiers over the unknown,
and the check-points, too many, so many to remember,
from the navel of Nimbia
to the bust of Bauchi,
Past the forest,
past the log greenness of Tigi,
To the lush valley
and the lustful hills and bends
of Hawan Kibo,
(many have gone on these bends)
Past Tahoss
by the colonial rail
Past Riyom, Vom and Jos...

A new energy ploughed into the vein
I am on the first lap of the coal-tar ...

Then the crazy convoy of campaigners, what mad rush?
They spoil the sight of busty mountains and tender trees

The road to Gombe is paved
with the reluctance of bridges and cattle
At Godon Waya, I behold the breasts
of table mountains, shrouded by the evening mist

They speak of the road as of a monster,
here I see a breathless woman spread endlessly,
a dark slim stretch of bitumen on the plateau,
her laps roughly used...

Through the crazed race, past Bauchi
and the numerous villages whistling by...
the fireflies accompany me
the checkpoints awaken me.

How quiet it is now
When the road ends...

I must dismount and go gently into the night.

Kiagbodo

(for J. P. Clark)

I am in the creek, on the Kiagbodo,
one lap of the course depth
to the mouth of the Forcados.

It was evening,
the river took my limbs and the children laughed
Their frolic and the fronds waved
as the paddler rowed to the riverbird's doorsteps.
We stepped over the bamboo thresh,
which held hyacinths at bay.

I am in the creek, on the Kiagbodo,
watching the ebbs return
from the market of waves.

And there, I prayed to the watery wind
for balance to my highland memory;
and there, moving frescoes,
men and women on wizened paddles,
voices and echoes on the creek serene;
there, the riverbird recounted a life in full tide;

...down there, two giant candles on iron stilts
following the sheen-path of fugitive oil.
Two giant thunders bellowing through the village night.
The carbon heat kissed my breath in the morning
I am scorched like the earth,
The sunbird and the river greet me still.

Scorched bank
I am in the creek, on the Kiagbodo,
Scorched bank, your armpit is all of oil-lamps
I am in the creek

river of history, travelling without maps
to your doorsteps, sitting by your shrine:

Riverbird, riverbird
Tell me more about your wondrous woes.

Riverbed, riverbed
Tell me more about your histories of scars.

Ukrainian Day

(a train poem)

The morning moon
red as the tiger's eye
followed us
through the huge pine
fingers of the forests,
from Lviv to Kyiv
in three tender days
I conquered your Cyrillic beauty,
timid to claim your tongue
I learn too to speak
in slow motion
You are the unforgettable breath
of the Poltva,
the rocks, and the chiselled stones.

The chiselled rocks, and the stones
of the Poltva.
You are the unforgettable breath
in slow motion
I learn too to speak
timid to claim your tongue
I conquered your Cyrillic beauty.
In three tender days
from Kyiv to Lviv
the fingers of the forests,
through the huge pine
followed us.
Red as the tiger's eye
Oh, the morning moon of my passion.

The curious glint in the eye
The dark alleys of your smiles
The eyelash of your laughters
The symphony of water running underneath...

Like Pushkin, I visit you, Lubny
I return with the unforgettable beauty of your land.

Lines from Palma de Mallorca

Poetry lives
in the olive mountain of Buger
of many tongues.
Away now
from the baptism
of my Mallorcan memory
Bathe me now, the recompense of remembrance.
* * *

In Valldemossa, Chopin and Sand.
One winter morning they made love
in the convent
and the mountain became summer.
And God wept.
Angels and mortals moaning in the convent...
* * *

In Deia, flowers bloom on mountains,
my blood boils by the foams,
Watching the full playfulness of waves
I drowned taking your image in tow.
* * *

It was a silent movie
Sharing poetry in prison
making music in the plenipotent house...

Fooled
by the eager orgy of eyes
and those voices that accompany the song, interns all.
Did Poetry go to prison on the island?
Poetry went to see people in the plenipotentiary...
* * *

Prayers for the weak; songs for the condemned...

Pain behind the manicured lens
And there's laughter too from the tiny window.

* * *

I come here not to die in your beauty
Palma, if I must sink in your waters
let it be in the froth of Estrella Damm
let it be in the stormy breeze of the last cup of the virgin wine
Let it be in your presence: crianza and reserva,
You are the authentic waters of pleasant taste.

Kwansaba I
(Lessons from a dream sequence)

Heroes do not write their own endings
Full moons do not kill the sky
Rivers do not bend in dry seasons
The whale's curse won't dry the oceans
The day's trouble won't kill the month
The lion's poverty won't kill his pride
The bride's beauty won't prolong the night.

Soft bite
(to PC, personal companion)

beyond the rivers of memory beyond
the hub of a thousand secrets and glitches
I love your bits and bytes,
and the binary punch captures it all...

scribbled, my fingers sing across the monitors of life,
these words strut, stream and sigh across the sea
in the silent hums of hard disks, in the full flight of the winged
hour
all our life is tied to these tiny things – open books & faceless
groups

all our life bound to things not green
yet moguls and hackers wield the battle-cry on a tender earth
we must kiss, kill or be killed, children of virtual hi-ways
chips aren't cheap again in the pawn shops of virus-mongers...

when this poem is done, and the batteries of our energies explode,
like the H-bomb, we shall not be saved on earth, in hell, or
heaven...
who, or what shall we delete; where, or when shall we repeat
the song of Origin: *Let there be light, without destruction!*

All of me is people
After the messages after a birthday

Friends, Compatriots, Netizens and Denizens of our song
Hear me, for I have held this breath of thanks for so long

This energy of love that filled my day
How can I this joyful glow repay

Your flow of wishes has not passed unfelt
For in your tsunami of prayers I am blest

Each utterance touches me, nerve, bone and blood
I, all the recipient of this human flood

I have lived a life simply, as God's sheep and father's rival
I have lived as if I would not be Tomorrow's survival

Hark, what does the bell of a birthday say:

> *Mortal, your day grows and ticks by*
> *Let it not be said that you didn't try*

When I am naked to want, warmth and life's riddle
I know indeed, as always: all of me is people.

Intimation of a final departure
(for Ayo Fadiran, Kados)

All birds will go home
Only the way and the wind
Is not certain.

Your fantasies still hang in the air
Fluttering wings, warm nests and other dreams
Everything now bloodied to a silence.

II
Ebbs

The poet

The poet too is a mobile prison,
the rough rhombus of colourful tales.

The poet is the flimsy energies of the blind seer
Free but chained to the recalcitrant image
of memory, of blood of birth and death
of the mating cry and the battle cry.

The poet is married to the rainbow of words...
Scavenger and hunted, also a lover loosed upon the world.

The poet is your voice, silenced but alive in the streets
the chameleon and the mask, the incurable child.

The blood and the wine of experience...
I think the poet is not
where there is nothing to live for.

Echoes of absence

In the year of the dying hyena
Every farmer becomes a hunter.

In the faint whispers of the wounded lion
Every hunter becomes the compound of courage.

In the hour of the dead buffalo
Every knife is the king of the slice.

When the river is licked dry by the sun
Every bird becomes a seasoned swimmer.

When the valley is flooded to the waist
Every tunnel also boasts like the river.

And when the carver departs, in search of forms
His drummer becomes the vendor of masques.

May these words weigh more than their echoes…
May the echoes travel beyond the sounds.

News from home

some fellows voted with slogans,
some vowed with pebbles and sticks
some found no voice,
so they murmured...
some melted with the lap of night
some lost their limbs to the lie
some lost their voices
because they licked the boot
still some wondered what why how
some still ignorant of the crude math...
some blew the fuse in the national circuit
some swallowed the incense of blood
some carried their placards to hapless gods
some cursed, some brayed, some prayed
some cried foul, safely from faraway lands.
now i know my country is bereaved
and it is the death of silence, forever.

Our fragments

inthebeginning, intheforgeintherafter, inthemesh
inthestitchinthemuseum, intheheatoffluentrivers
inthedanceintheindigo, inthecanefieldsintheopencity...
inthepredictabilityofthehour, intheroughopenneckoftherace
inthegaggleofnight, inthesplutterofdawn, inthebreathoftheliving
our argument is splintered into the many parts of the crab.

My country is bereaved

we have just survived
another lap of war.
the chivalrous killers
are waiting outside
sharing their spoils.
they make jest of my people
the ones who live
from dust to mouth every day.
it is a war
against the poor man's belly
it is a war
addressed to the wretched
by those we gave our votes freely
forgetting the fears
they will become dictators.

now is the season of blood
children and old women
maimed by fresh bullets
borrowed from foreign lands.
the blood continues to flow
a new smokescreen of vipers
playing the violins for us to dance
by force by force by force.

we who are serial casualties say,
the last drop of the last man
will speak for us
for we are washed beyond
the cabal crookedness in the air.
the tribal marks of war are here
the subterfuge season is here.

we who feed now
from the howling winds
we exhale and say,
we shall survive the tyrant poison.
We shall survive the ammonia of hate.

Three desperations

There are those who bled, silently, on the way to general damnation.

There are those who fled, by many routes, into the corners of their skins.

There are those who fed only, who fed on the rot of this land.

Sniper

Soweto & Freetown

A survivor, scarred by years of poachers, whispered to her rapist:
I, too, am pained by the paralysis of diseased histories
I forgive you.
I forgive you as the sun forgives the storms.
Your unspoken words already heal me,
And I can no longer watch you twitch in blood.

Abidjan & Abuja

We have combed the cobwebs of our differences
We should forget the aroma of foreign slogans
We can no longer eat the grapes of red dust.
Let us go, you and I, to the brew of new dances.

Darfur & Juba

I am the remaining sore in the heart...

Swing the sword in the name of your holiness
Or in the triumphant foolery of the tribe
Swing, swing the battle axe at your neighbour's tongue
Serve her blood to your hungry dogs,
and say prayers to your God in the next hour
Swing, swing the curse of locusts over the land.

I am the last seed of these empty barns.

This house full of noise

This house will not fall or break
This house too full of noise and fury
This house that spins on the pin of our pains
This house will not collapse on its own.

We did not choose the land before it chose us
We hugged our fate into the night into the dawn.

This house will not fall or break
This house too full of noise and fury
This house that spins on the pin of our pains
This house will not collapse on its own.

The cabinet is on fire, the shrine is looted
We will not faint at the smell of death.

This house will not fall or break
This house too full of noise and fury
This house that spins on the pin of our pains
This house will not collapse on its own.

We have been fed on the sucrose of shame
We have been dissolved in cubes of lies

This house will not fall or break
This house too full of noise and fury
This house that spins on the pin of our pains
This house will not collapse on its own.

Listen to the heartbeat of ants
Listen to the desires of bees and birds.

Listen to the laughter of rivers in full flight
Listen to the common cries of remnant voices.

This house will not fall or break
This house too full of noise and fury
This house built on the menstrual love of warriors
This house will not die less we die.

Run, country, run

The flood is still rising...
Blood still dripping from the paintings
In our museum of misery...

Run, country, run

The exhibitions of fire still burning
The fairy tales of peace
In the flair of bombs and abduction...

Run, country, run

We have put a curse on the household of graft
We have followed the thieves to the lip of the gallows

Run, country, run

We have set flames to the barn of ignorance
We have sent termites and locusts in the path of greed.

Into the fire
Into the fire
Into the waters
Into the waters
Be healed, be healed. Run, country, run.

It is you

It is you
who told the toad how to spit on the lion's grave.
It is you who stole the wind from the parrot's breath.
It is you who craved the gust of ash on our valiant forge
It is you, the portfolio of pus.

Where the wind is absent
the charcoal burns slowly, to its own death.
It is you who brought the weevil into the cotton yard.
Oh, the weaver's fingers pine in the absence of yarns
It is you it is you... it is you.

The toad in the grave, the weevil in the barn.
You burst into the market like *Sonponno*, god of pox
Only the sacrifice remains in the square.
It is you who brought locusts and silence to the ceremony,
a faggot of ants in the burial of lizards.

Now my pyramid of words is a trap-
ezium, is a trap in the open museum.
It is you
The singer must seethe his tongue
in the medusa moment, it is you

Snakes
spikes and nails
in the path of dance,
it is you
who brought this gift of a curse.

Counterfeit

You wasted no time teaching me how to be rich
Or richer in the grabbing game.

I am the stark fish in your net, oh phisher of men.
You must save me or shave me now…

My reply is late because a terrible thing happened.
Thunderstorms and tornadoes destroyed our roads.

Tens of our satellites fell into the lagoon. A great havoc it was.
Our cables dead, the transfer you want must be delayed.

You asked for details but I forgot to tell
Our website is stranded in the middle of the road

I am the next-of-kin to the commandeer of bonds
And my uncle is the sole janitor to our national treasury

I am here seated in my worry that I might lose your offer
And I wonder if you could send me some money, euro or dollar.

While we wait, I can teach you a thing to bite
For I can give as much as you receive

Will you be surprised that I hold a degree in Law,
from the Faculty of Chemistry, first class Fellow

So if you wish too to be wise like me
I can find admission for you at UNIPETROL

My country's first, yet to be copied
The logo is, labour is the medicine of dearth.

I shall waste no time teaching you how to be poor
Or poorer in the grabbing game.

City of prose

Not every sonnet comes
from the heart of a lover
Not every ode
is a lode of logic
Not every song
has a praise name
Not every limb
knows how
to steal a dance.

In the city of prose, every word is a knife in the vicious game.
In the city of prose, every knife is a word to the hilt. In the city
Of prose, a spade is called by its dirty name. In the city of prose.

We are the rage...

We have been scorched so many times
Like the fate of the multitude...
an armada of fire angry at our dreams.

Engulfed by the songs of war, and awakening
we are the many tongues of the forked river,
we want a voice...

We are the ones whose roads spread
and scatter into many paths; we are blessed but lost
in the numerous tracks to our bloody wars.

We, guardians of carnivals and songs:
we are the rage in fire's tongue
we are the fire in beauty's eye.

We are the beauty in the land's ugliness
we are the land beneath the dancer's feet
we are the dancers in the trance.

We are the trance in the rain, and we are the rains
in the lust of heat, we are the heat of a thousand storms.
And we are the many dreams out of a single slumber.

We stoke we seek we live we lie,
We die, and wake again, just like the moon in your eye
We are the inheritors of the rage.

So what will your hawks do to the tortoise gait?
What will your hawks do to our porcupine fate?
We are the rage of deferred dreams...

We are the earth, the sea and the suns of this land.

At last poetry is on the streets

I
in darkness i write these lines
i do not see the fingers that scribble
but my heart purrs on the page for you
i know the sun is still up outside.

II
in this frail hour there are many pretenders
i shall not fall to the jest of midnight silences
i shall not bow to the curve of colourful cowards
i will not stop until they look the sun in the eye.

III

the waters dragged the ground, roots and all
the fires dragged the forests, roots and all
the winds have no hands the river has no legs
the waters dragged our shame to the earth's end.

IV

i hear everything which moves, and dies is a target
one ballot to one bullet is the sum of our budget
as in the days of the junta, there's a regime of cheetahs
as in the years of the hyena, blood is let loose...

V

if you feel the flesh of my voice in the violence
please pass my prayer to the patriarchs of our pains
when they see blood again on the streets
it will be from the arteries of their children.

VI

so i stopped writing while the earth quakes
i do not see the hand that pulled the veil
i see the sun, the moon and the stars in embrace
today, tomorrow, the tremor of words will pull the trigger.

VII
at last poetry is on the streets...

The fire next time

Let us pause again
and count our fragments of fear.

Let us pause
and count the death of dreams.

They have called you to the praise of hate
They will teach you to stab your brother.

They have fed you on phosphates of fire
You must put a grim tongue on the green anthem.

They will sew a blood of mustards
And tell you it is the seed of sunflowers.

And they will give you the axe
And tell you to swing it as song.

They say laughter is lunacy
And anguish is also a kind of laughter...

Now you walk on a tornado of nails
You are the evidence of the fear.

> *Here is the conclave of vultures.*
> *Here is the concourse of crooks.*
> *Here is a communion of tears.*
> *Here is the poisoned pool.*

There will be silence after the mortars have spoken
There will be silence behind the barbed wires.

Now you must consume the tornado or be consumed
You must break the silence and dare the fire.

So when the whirlwind breaks again
Do not fall to the fragments of fire.

Say no, to the fire next time
Say no, to the fire, next time.

I have seen dead bones rise

After the waters raged
Nothing's left but silence and sorrow
After the waters rose,
Nothing's left standing, only
only the wind's breath
clung to the fallen bridge.

The fathers have disappeared....
Gone with the ominous night.
Gone, with the anger of waters
The mothers have clothed their heads in ash.
We asked to teach the children new songs of laughter
Now they munch the sourness of wilted corns.

I have searched the entrails of our tale
Our narrative has caught fire
Our narrative is wilted
in the shrivelled lips of orphans
After the waters raged,
nobody thinks tomorrow will come.

But I have seen dead bones rise.
I have seen the prison walls of closed minds fall
I have seen the sun rise in the depth of night
And in the huge appetite of hungry deserts
I have heard the gurgles of oases...
I have seen flooded fields smile in verdant colours.

After the rivers' rage
In the aftermath of acid rains
Tomorrow's sun will rise
Accompanied by the rays of deodorant winds,
Accompanied by the fruity fingers of naked flowers.
Tomorrow's sun will rise
I have seen dead bones rise.

III
Flows

Sea of my mind
(for mother)

Naked, there is a silence here that makes loudness die
Naked, my heart splashed by the twisted sea in your eye.

The rocks roll gently,
Your voice going faintly.

I am listening to the signs under the undergrowth
You whispered me to life and now I hear your last breath.

There is a silence here that makes the heart bleed
Your body is a ferment of tattoos, beads and slow speed.

Fairer than the oil of gods, you're the last incense
I am lost to the dream, to time and the mortal sense.

Naked, washed smooth by the stones in your eyes
Naked, the day bright, you looked beyond me into the skies...

Naked like a sailor, I come to you, travelling the length of earth.
I greet the winds in your face, I see the unfurled seeds of a new birth.

I touch the sea, capture the passions of natal fever
Naked, my fingers fishing for pulse, it shall be warm forever.

Mother, I arrive, naked to your last prayer
I bring you the vows of an everlasting fire.

The longest night breaks and you become the goddess

Naked, every day I drink water, I remember you.

I am the one you breathe

I am the one you breathe
the open air breeze
on your tongue
I am the double roll
on the fluent lip
The whisper
in your heart's silence
Singer of unwritten notes
sensate, quiver of breaths
Eternal summer in your soul
Say my name now
I am with you. Say my name.

I spread my thoughts
like the washerman
In the open air
on these green grass
on the lines
Above the dirty gutters
and the sewers,
away from the spiralled soots
Spread, spread now
like the wings of the sunbird
I spread the seeds
the sheets all for you,
now naked to the bones
I kill the secrets and the fears
Say my name now
I am with you. Say my name.

I am like your tongue
the roll of waterfalls

Paddle me right
and survive the trip;
put a tear in the saddle
and bear the accident
of the fatal fall...
Say my name now,
I am with you. Say my name.

Now I compare you with the skin of rivers

The river is in my hand; my hand is the river,
stretched as far as the liquid dream.

I, sojourner on the crest of the deep
I, the water bird covered in the brocade of your gaze.

There's a fitfulness in my heart only your blood can cure
I compare you to the joyful fever of the harvester's fingers.

I compare you to the ebb and the skin of the rivers
I compare you now to the limbless aura of the sky.

This is the depth of our everest love, this is the valley
of our delta dreams, this is the futa djallon flow of our waists.

Stand still, my love, let ours be the bellow of plaintive nights.

Now I compare you with the colour of the gentle waves.
The earth wants the flamenco feel of the wind
But the wind tells the earth to stand still...

Stand still, love, let ours be the night of tender winds...

If you should hear a raspberry echo in your heart
it is my blood that flows there. Live it.
The hand that touches you is a river...

Sky scenes

Your cloud is a chameleon of intrigues
Bright now, then blue, dark and a light redness
a geography of sensations,
a chameleon,
bowels of a thousand lights
a wide blue ocean of fluttering wings
Sometimes too, your cheeks are a permanent exile of rains.

Now I see the threat of typhoons in your eyes
Come river, come rain, my imaginary canoe is ready.
I shall survive the storms.

Your name is the perfume of night

Seeing you as the silhouette of night;
as if your name is singed to the perfume of simple dreams.

You are the syllables I have lusted for,
all the eagerness of my trembling lips.

My fingers find your shadow and hang in mid-air,
you become the chiselled pillar of salt.

How do I say the magical word, or touch the waves of your skin;
how do I survive the brink of your paralysis, dream-woman?

Though far from you, I behold them all,
the graceful gait, the bright breath, the sweetener smile...

The wind that touches your cheek this morning
Is mine is mine is mine...

I am the night; you are the star above, oil of my mangrove fire
Your name is the perfume of night...

River, take my heart

Tonight is the perfect night,
Calm when the moon rests on my shoulder
Calm in spite of the many storms within...

Tonight the sun and the moon mate
in the river-bed of our breaths
Take my heart, river of tremors

Tonight, there's an earthquake in my heart,
a sea swells from within and here,
Where your words touch me beyond words...

What binds us now, what binds us now?

I do not know
A honeyed lump
stumbles in my throat.

Tomorrow will come
and the moon will desert the sun
as the sun deserts the stars.

When I leave what would you remember me for?

Tonight, I remember you as the rope that binds
I remember you as the ventricle of passions.

You are the breath that stems from my mouth
You are the eye of the northern star showing me the way...

So, you may go as the revolving sun,
your heat remains in the vein

You may leave as the spangling star,
you remain as the beautiful scar on my skin

Tonight, I remember you
as the bank remembers the receding river

Tonight, I remember you
Always waiting, ever longing…

I have crossed
seven dangerous rivers
for you
I remember
every gesture,
every argument
and every tenderness
you give
I remember
every thing
I miss about you…
To arrive
at this night,
Tonight
is the perfect night.

Breathing

I like your body breathing...
I like your breeding,
your breath in and out

the heaving of our crested love
the panting speech of your eyes
the vanilla pout of your lips

And I like it when the wind howls your name in my ears.

Even now the butterfly that perches on my tree
Leaves a pollen in the garden, its talcum is the colour of your
face.

My pity for the dancing partner who beholds your limbs only
but not your sensation.

My pity to the one who sees you everyday but does not feel.
Like me.

Let all the maidens come to the banks of the Niger
It is you my paddle will touch.

Long is the silence of deep oceans.
Quick is the anger of the panther.
Fresh and fast is the life of the morning dew.

As these, you are the flesh of my fate.

In the groove of the silence
In the tongue of the panting
In the bones of your shadow
I will be content to lose my name.

I like your breeding.

I like your adverbs

I like your adverbs.
Still, you are the same one
who pelted my heart with stones
soft as feathers, still.

I like your adverbs.
Whatever, the sun always shines
bright and hot, where it makes a home
in your eyes, whatever.

I like your adverbs
Because, you're the one who walks in my sleep
and I don't want to wake from it all,
because I like your adverbs.

I like your adverbs when...
When I think of you as legion
as the dress of the chameleon
numerous as the onion's rags...

I like your adverbs, perhaps.
I may be the absence
that caused the pain, perhaps
the bee that missed the pollen,

I like your adverbs.
Cursed to mourn the sweet verb,
I will find you. As the moon finds the earth.
As the river finds the bank.

Still, whatever, because, perhaps
Still, I like all the adverbs in you...

Clinging

Now the blink and breath of my day
is draped in the lightness of your skin
As thunder to rain, as rain
to the magic of clouds, as the clouds
to migrant men and birds, as men too
to their shadows, and birds to the buffalo trail
I am clung,
sewn
roundly staked,
sacrificed
to the very pores of your presence.

Swallowed
in the tongue of your fire
Tied
to the flair of your river's limbs
A certain numbness overwhelms where you are.

There's nothing more,
no thing,
no song,
no food,
no water,
no thirst
but you.

There's no beautiful poem like you...

You came shining
like the transparency of day
And Silence took hold of me
Awe stitched to my wondering eye
I have forgotten the murmurs and
what I whispered into your ears now
But I remembered watching my legs
lead in your direction
Like the bee to its pollen
Like the sea to its bank...
I wanted a simple brush
with the wind of your skin
The inscrutable dews
of your virgin smile
And when finally you turned to speak
The hall stuttered out of silence,
And the wind heard your call...
You're the awesome sea,
the captive harbour.

I yield now to the nuclear flood in your eyes.
You're the poem not yet written
waiting to be ...

Abebi

Tonight your voice accompanies me
You touch me from this distance
As the hands of rain on jubilant soils.
Parched, I am perched
on the sole dream of eternal remembrance.

Tonight all the saints and spirits bless you, my mother.
I see your victory above the vanity.

I give you

I give you
    a thousand metaphors,
a million metonyms
    of flowers
      that never wither,
I give you
    a billion baskets
of bounteous wishes,
    as brilliant as day
I give you
    one sun, many moons and
      several stars of alliteration
I give you
    the symphony
of decorated nights
    on Christmas season
I give you
    the warmth of my tropical sun,
I give you
    the personifications of joy,
in your hour of hesitations
    and worries, in your lonely time,
I send you
    the tumulus of the wind's embrace
because I am in the air you breathe.

Kwansaba II
(for Eugene B. Redmond)

Once we combed the routes and spaces
Where our fathers' sweats became the rivers
Unknown, where their dreams melted into pains
We shared the routes of golden returns
You became the acolyte of new unions
Between Ibadan and East St. Louis alive
Now you have become a legend, forever.

Every. Thing. Matters.
(Bremen poem)

You said nothing really matters when we are dancing
Not even the spread of your wings
Nor the flutter in my heart
The simple spin of the waist to the spirit of dance

Everything matters my love
Everything like your breath
Everything like your magic
Everything like your curve
Every. Thing. Matters.

I have held your breath in these hands before
And you know when my heart starts pumping
You are the key to the rhythm
Nothing matters in your libation

Nothing really matters when the rhythm of dance descends
Because you're both the dance, and the song.

Resolve

Oh lucky hour, oh stretched second

Give me the lavender smell of night.

Give me the limbless stealth of winds,

Give me the teeth of valiant bees

Give me the vulcan gush of tornadoes,

Give me fire,

Give me love.

May the wind follow my plaintiff wish

When I hold the throat of the road
I do not want to return
I bear the sea in my mind
When I touch the waist of the highway
I want to go with the dawn
Supplicant to the elixir of impatient limbs
I have set my head on the plinth of long paths
I have tasted the totem milk of the clan
Willed to the fate of sparrows
I become the lot of salt, flowing in the seduction of rivers
When the road calls and the highway beckons
I go like the deaf dog, willed to the fate of rivers
When the road opens and the highway invites
May the sun hear my prayers
May the wind be gentle to my dreams
May the wind follow my plaintiff wish.

Recessional

Keǹgbè Ọ̀rọ̀

Bẹ́ẹ̀ni ọ̀rọ̀ ń bẹ ńílé Baba tó bí mi lọ́mọ, tó ńmí túke túke
Ògidi ọ̀rọ̀, àabọ̀ ọ̀rọ̀, ọ̀rọ̀ kà ǹ kà, ọ̀rọ̀ bínńtín...
Ọ̀rọ̀ àsírí, ọ̀rọ̀ gbékùn àgbà bí ọlẹ̀ d'àgbà.

Ọ̀rọ̀ bẹ́, ọ̀rọ̀ ya, ọ̀rọ̀ gbé
Ọ̀rọ̀ tí ń gbé ni mì bí ibú Olókun
Ọ̀rọ̀ tí ń nani ní patiyẹ léńje léńje.

Mo wí ná, ọ̀rọ̀ ń bẹ ńílé Baba tó bí mi lọ́mọ
Ọ̀rọ̀ ní î gb'órin n'íyàwó, àwọn orin a sì má ṣ'alárinà ọ̀rọ̀.

Ọ̀rọ̀ já, ọ̀rọ̀ so, ọ̀rọ̀ wú, ọ̀rọ̀ bẹ́
Ọ̀rọ̀ la fi ńjagun, ọ̀rọ̀ la fi ńṣẹ́gun

Ọ̀rọ̀ tí kò l'éegun tí ń gun ni wọ ṣóńṣó ara
Ọ̀rọ̀ tí kò léyìn tí î boni mọ́lẹ̀ bí tamọtiye.

Ọ̀rọ̀ tí kò lọ́wọ́, tí î gbá ni lójú bíi akika.
Ọ̀rọ̀ já, ọ̀rọ̀ so, ọ̀rọ̀ wú, ọ̀rọ̀ bẹ́.

Ọ̀rọ̀ já ọ̀rọ̀ jó, ọ̀rọ̀ le, ọ̀rọ̀ là
Ọ̀rọ̀ dé, ọ̀rọ̀ dà, ọ̀rọ̀ a sì má dà wààrà bí òjò.

Ọ̀rọ̀ bẹ́ bí ọlọ́kùnrùn ilé ọ̀ọ́kán
Ọ̀rọ́ di iyán, ọ̀rọ́ di iyan, ọ̀rọ́ fọ́ yánpọnyánrin sílẹ̀ láàrin wọn.

Ọ̀rògodogànyin ọ̀rọ̀
Ọ̀rọ̀ já, ọ̀rọ̀ so, ọ̀rọ̀ wú, ọ̀rọ̀ bẹ́ẹ́
Ọ̀rọ̀ wí, ọ̀rọ̀ wó, ọ̀rọ́ ṣí, ọ̀rọ̀ dí. Ọ̀rọ̀ rò! Ọ̀rọ̀ rọ̀ọ̀, bí ọjọ́ là.

In the barrel of words*

...the word is perched in father's chest, panting heavily
Half-word, full utter, huge, heaving and tiny words
Underground, unknown like the two-day old foetus.

You bend, you tear, you break
You swallow as the watery jaw of Olokun
Is it not you, whip in the waist of the child?

I say the word is perched in my father's nest
The word marries the song, the song is midwife of words.

You break, you tie, you swell, you burst
The word is sword against power.

The word boneless, it pricks the flesh to depths.
The word toothless, it bears the fangs of ants.

The word armless, it blasts the face like the hedgehog
The word breaks, the word ties, the word swells, the word bursts.

The word tears, it pounces; the word hardens, the word heals
The word comes tumbling like the sea of rains.

The word stinks like the familiar destitute
The word is pounded into a compound of chaos.

Incubus and Succubus in flight
You break you tie; you swell and burst again.
You speak you slumber; you open and close now.
You descend, you rise. You, rise, you descend.

My word breaks, it breaks like the face of dawn.

---

* Self-translation of the Yoruba text, "Kèǹgbè Ọ̀rọ̀", originally presented
at the 12th International Festival of Mediterranean Poetry in Palma de
Mallorca (June 2, 2010).

Kraftgriots

Also in the series (POETRY) *continued*

Joe Ushie: *A Reign of Locusts* (2004)
Paulina Mabayoje: *The Colours of Sunset* (2004)
Segun Adekoya: *Guinea Bites and Sahel Blues* (2004)
Ebi Yeibo: *Maiden Lines* (2004)
Barine Ngaage: *Rhythms of Crisis* (2004)
Funso Aiyejina: *I,The Supreme & Other Poems* (2004)
'Lere Oladitan: *Boolekaja: Lagos Poems 1* (2005)
Seyi Adigun: *Bard on the Shore* (2005)
Famous Dakolo: *A Letter to Flora* (2005)
Olawale Durojaiye: *An African Night* (2005)
G. 'Ebinyo Ogbowei: *let the honey run & other poems* (2005)
Joe Ushie: *Popular Stand & Other Poems* (2005)
Gbemisola Adeoti: *Naked Soles* (2005)
Aj. Dagga Tolar: *This Country is not a Poem* (2005)
Tunde Adeniran: *Labyrinthine Ways* (2006)
Sophia Obi: *Tears in a Basket* (2006)
Tonyo Biriabebe: *Undercurrents* (2006)
Ademola O. Dasylva: *Songs of Odamolugbe* (2006), winner, 2006 ANA/Cadbury
    poetry prize
George Ehusani: *Flames of Truth* (2006)
Abubakar Gimba: *This Land of Ours* (2006)
G. 'Ebinyo Ogbowei: *the heedless ballot box* (2006)
Hyginus Ekwuazi: *Love Apart* (2006), winner, 2007 ANA/NDDC Gabriel Okara
    poetry prize and winner, 2007 ANA/Cadbury poetry prize
Abubakar Gimba: *Inner Rumblings* (2006)
Albert Otto: *Letters from the Earth* (2007)
Aj. Dagga Tolar: *Darkwaters Drunkard* (2007)
Idris Okpanachi: *The Eaters of the Living* (2007), winner, 2008 ANA/Cadbury
    poetry prize
Tubal-Cain: *Mystery in Our Stream* (2007), winner, 2006 ANA/NDDC Gabriel
    Okara poetry prize
John Iwuh: *Ashes & Daydreams* (2007)
Sola Owonibi: *Chants to the Ancestors* (2007)
Doutimi Kpakiama: *Salute to our Mangrove Giants* (2008)
Halima M. Usman: *Spellbound* (2008)
Hyginus Ekwuazi: *Dawn Into Moonlight: All Around Me Dawning* (2008), winner,
    2008 ANA/NDDC Gabriel Okara poetry prize
Ismail Bala Garba & Abdullahi Ismaila (eds.): *Pyramids: An Anthology of Poems
    from Northern Nigeria* (2008)
Denja Abdullahi: *Abuja Nunyi (This is Abuja)* (2008)
Japhet Adeneye: *Poems for Teenagers* (2008)
Seyi Hodonu: *A Tale of Two in Time (Letters to Susan)* (2008)
Ibukun Babarinde: *Running Splash of Rust and Gold* (2008)
Chris Ngozi Nkoro: *Trails of a Distance* (2008)

(POETRY) *continued*

Tunde Adeniran: *Beyond Finalities* (2008)
Abba Abdulkareem: *A Bard's Balderdash* (2008)
Ifeanyi D. Ogbonnaya: *... And Pigs Shall Become House Cleaners* (2008)
Ebinyo Ogbowei: *the town crier's song* (2009)
Ebinyo Ogbowei: *song of a dying river* (2009)
Sophia Obi-Apoko: *Floating Snags* (2009)
Akachi Adimora-Ezeigbo: *Heart Songs* (2009), winner, 2009 ANA/Cadbury poetry prize
Hyginus Ekwuazi: *The Monkey's Eyes* (2009)
Seyi Adigun: *Prayer for the Mwalimu* (2009)
Faith A. Brown: *Endless Season* (2009)
B.M. Dzukogi: *Midnight Lamp* (2009)
B.M. Dzukogi: *These Last Tears* (2009)
Chimezie Ezechukwu: *The Nightingale* (2009)
Ummi Kaltume Abdullahi: *Tiny Fingers* (2009)
Ismaila Bala & Ahmed Maiwada (eds.): *Fireflies: An Anthology of New Nigerian Poetry* (2009)
Eugenia Abu: *Don't Look at Me Like That* (2009)
Data Osa Don-Pedro: *You Are Gold and Other Poems* (2009)
Sam Omatseye: *Mandela's Bones and Other Poems* (2009)
Sam Omatseye: *Dear Baby Ramatu* (2009)
C.O. Iyimoga: *Fragments in the Air* (2010)
Bose Ayeni-Tsevende: *Streams* (2010)
Seyi Hodonu: *Songs from My Mother's Heart (2010)*, winner ANA/NDDC Gabriel Okara poetry prize, 2010
Akachi Adimora-Ezeigbo: *Waiting for Dawn* (2010)
Hyginus Ekwuazi: *That Other Country* (2010), winner, ANA/Cadbury poetry prize, 2010
Tosin Otitoju: *Comrade* (2010)
Arnold Udoka: *Poems Across Borders* (2010)
Arnold Udoka: *The Gods Are So Silent & Other Poems* (2010)
Abubakar Othman: *The Passions of Cupid* (2010)
Okinba Launko: *Dream-Seeker on Divining Chain* (2010)
'kufre ekanem: *the ant eaters* (2010)
McNezer Fasehun: *Ever Had a Dear Sister* (2010)
Baba S. Umar: *A Portrait of My People* (2010)
Gimba Kakanda: *Safari Pants* (2010)
Sam Omatseye: *Lion Wind & Other Poems* (2011)
Ify Omalicha: *Now that Dreams are Born* (2011)
Karo Okokoh: *Souls of a Troubadour* (2011)
Ada Onyebuenyi, Chris Ngozi Nkoro, Ebere Chukwu (eds): *Uto Nka: An Anthology of Literature for Fresh Voices* (2011)
Mabel Osakwe: *Desert Songs of Bloom* (2011)
Pious Okoro: *Vultures of Fortune & Other Poems* (2011)
Godwin Yina: *Clouds of Sorrows* (2011)

Nnimmo Bassey: *I Will Not Dance to Your Beat* (2011)
Denja Abdullahi: *A Thousand Years of Thirst* (2011)
Enoch Ojotisa: *Commoner's Speech* (2011)
Rowland Timi Kpakiama: *Bees and Beetles* (2011)
Niyi Osundare: *Random Blues* (2011)
Lawrence Ogbo Ugwuanyi: *Let Them Not Run* (2011)
Saddiq M. Dzukogi: *Canvas* (2011)
Arnold Udoka: *Running with My Rivers* (2011)
Olusanya Bamidele: *Erased Without a Trace* (2011)
Olufolake Jegede: *Treasure Pods* (2012)
Karo Okokoh: *Songs of a Griot* (2012), winner. ANA/NDDC Gabriel Okara
    poetry prize, 2012
Musa Idris Okpanachi: *From the Margins of Paradise* (2012)
John Martins Agba: *The Fiend and Other Poems* (2012)
Sunnie Ododo: *Broken Pitchers* (2012)
'Kunmi Adeoti: *Epileptic City* (2012)
Ibiwari Ikiriko: *Oily Tears of the Delta* (2012)
Bala Dalhatu: *Moonlights* (2012)
Karo Okokoh: *Manna for the Mind* (2012)
Chika O. Agbo: *The Fury of the Gods* (2012)
Emmanuel C. S. Ojukwu: *Beneath the Sagging Roof* (2012)
Amirikpa Oyigbenu: *Cascades and Flakes* (2012)
Ebi Yeibo: *Shadows of the Setting Sun* (2012)
Chikaoha Agoha: *Shreds of Thunder* (2012)
Mark Okorie: *Terror Verses* (2012)
Clemmy Igwebike-Ossi: *Daisies in the Desert* (2012)
Idris Amali: *Back Again (At the Foothills of Greed)* (2012)
Akachi Adimora-Ezeigbo: *Dancing Masks* (2013)